DELI DITTIES

DELI DITTIES

MAGGIE LAWRENCE and KEITH WILSHIRE

Published in 2023 by Margaret E Lawrence

ISBN: 978-0-6451303-4-8

Copyright © Maggie Lawrence and Keith Wilshire, 2023
People photography © 2023. Riverview Coffee Collective, Lane Cove
Nature photographs Copyright © Maggie Lawrence

Front and back cover designs Kindle Direct Publishing.

A collection of limericks and poems developed
after a group of friends began meeting
for coffee at York's Corner deli in the
Sydney suburb of Lane Cove.

Written by Maggie Lawrence
and Keith Wilshire.

Additional poems from Harold Brown,
Linda Hardy, Ted Rule and Marea McDonnell

For Paul

KEITH

THE RIVERVIEW COFFEE COLLECTIVE

We are the Riverview Coffee Collective.

We sometimes speak with lots of invective.

Give us a cup from Tony's beans

Then we remember all of our teens.

Until it all dissipates leaving us restive.

Tony runs the cafe with aplomb.

He has a new barista

His name is Tom.

It all started with a man called Paul.

He was a TV man who stood tall.

Keith and Harold are usually there.

Maggie comes down and we find her a chair.

 ****

KEITH

THE RIVERVIEW COFFEE COLLECTIVE

John enjoys the company for sure.

He comes along when he hasn't a chore.

Linda H has become a regular.

Linda N makes it when not in Tilba.

Kim we see once in a while.

Stephen calls in with a smile.

Louise has come along a few times.

Her father Ted can make a few rhymes.

We haven't seen Kelly for a while

Even though we love hearing her sing with a smile.

Elizabeth once had a dog called Maggie.

She drops by for a cup when she feels saggy.

 ****

KEITH

THE RIVERVIEW COFFEE COLLECTIVE

We sometimes meet Marea
When she's not busy with her career.
Cynthia likes our café and comes on down
When she's not too busy running around.

We've met a man called Ted.
His dog has a happy head.

There is a young woman named Kim.
Who can eat all day, and stay slim.

My apologies to anyone I've forgotten.
My mind these days is a little rotten.
But the coffee helps me to see
That I don't need to rely on ChatGPT.

KEITH

WHAT'S IT FOR?

Six months I've been paying for the gym.
Promising myself I'd actually go in.
Went there, and now I'm really sore.
I wonder what it's really all for.

CLATTER

My denture has come loose in the middle of dinner.
I'm stuck in a bind - am I going to get thinner?
Raised my fork with a sweet carrot attached.
Savouring the sight of it steamed and blanched.
Opened my mouth with great anticipation.
I shock my friends with a clattering expectoration.
I've lost it again.
Oh what a pain.

MAGGIE

YORK'S CORNER CAFÉ

We like to go to Tony's.
It's our special time each day.
He sells all kinds of goodies
That we sometimes take away.
He'll remember your name
From the last time you came.
And if you only buy a coffee it will suffice.

NO TURNING BACK

Coffee isn't just good.
It's really great.
And drinking it seems to be my fate.
I used to like tea.
Never touched coffee.
But now I've got the coffee taste
There's no turning back.
It's far too late.

MAGGIE

LANE CAVOODLE

On Sydney's lower north shore, you'll find Lane Cove.
I am pleased I chose it for my abode.
You're spoiled for choice for places to drink and eat.
Many lovely trees to shelter from the heat.

People travel all over Sydney to eat at the canopy.
Fine dining is in abundance there you see.
And there are health facilities everywhere.
You don't need to travel far for excellent healthcare.

There are glorious trails in the bush for a walk.
Parrots, Magpies and Cockatoos enjoy a squawk.
At Blackman park I even heard a whip bird.
To be so close to the city it's quite absurd.

Although surrounded by bush and gorgeous flowers
You can get to the city in just a quarter of an hour.
You'll see lots of dogs with names that end in oodle.
It's why we call Lane Cove - Lane Cavoodle.

One of the many gorgeous bush tracks in Lane Cove

Jacaranda path in Lane Cove

KEITH

THE DENTIST

I'm off to the dentist once again.
It's a funny place, promising pain
And blessed relief as the ultimate gain.
Along the journey are high pitched drills,
Multiple needles and anti-biotic pills.
I hope this is my last visit to the devil's
-- Chair --.

ELECTRICITY

Electricity is a buzz.
Although I'm afraid, because
What happens when it disappears?
And I'm left with only my fears.
Because then everything, stops it does.

KEITH

BLANKET DESIRE

With winter comes our blanket desire.
To cover up and be by the fire.
As a child I would rush to play soccer
But now, more likely to be a blogger.
I collect old wood to burn in the fire
Then bask in the bubble of our glowing pyre.

KEITH

A WINTER'S DAY IN NORMANHURST

Sitting on the carpet in the hall.
Feeling the wintry warmth lying on the floor
Of the sun streaming through the glass front door.
Hearing the Kookaburras laughing in the trees.
My sister saying they were laughing with me.
For so long I believed they knew my thoughts.
I have always felt affinity with the laughing cohorts.
They are so loud and bold, high in the trees.
In my autistic silence they offered great relief.
Even to this day I can vividly recall
That sunny winter day lying in the hall.

KEITH

UN-RHYMED

I've had a cold (or was it COVID)?
I've been cuddled up at home wrapped and doona'd.
I'm wondering which genome of bugs
Has festooned all through my head.

These bugs have stolen my rhyming.
And filled my nose with junk.
But now it's dinner time.
Somehow, I cooked something with ease.
I wonder what sort of funk I've created.
With all that cheese.

MABLE (with assistance from Harold B)

Sitting here at the table.
Thinking of you Mable.
You've forsaken me.
Not sitting on my knee.
I'd chase you, if I was able.

Maggie

YORK'S CORNER FRIENDS

Marinko comes when his dad is okay.
He doesn't always stay to buy a latte.
He looks after his dad like a really good son.
He enjoys coming out when we see the sun.

Anne Maree doesn't come along.
She stays at home to write a new song.
Her work is going very well.
Her focus is there. We can tell.

I've got to know a lady called Kelly.
She comes to the Riverview Deli.
She sings like a lark.
Goes home in the dark.
And we've seen her singing on the telly.

 ****

MAGGIE

YORK'S CORNER FRIENDS

I know a man called John.
His surname is Armstrong.
To Tony's delight he buys a skimmed flat white.
And stays at the cafe quite long.

On a rare occasion we catch up with Liz.
She comes to the cafe if not too biz.
She only drinks tea - not Tony's coffee.
It's nice when she comes. It is.

Mary came along from time to time.
She is very witty when someone isn't kind.
A rude lady once poked her in the side. She said,
'Better check your broomstick parked outside.'

Harold dresses with a great sense of style.
We see him coming and break into a smile.
'You're a true English gent.' Maggie tells our Harry.
'No wonder your Eva wanted you to marry.'

 ****

MAGGIE

YORK'S CORNER FRIENDS

Linda N comes to see us
When she's not down the coast.
Her herbal teas we like the most.
And Ted pays us a visit with his dancing dog Xander.
He jumps for sheer joy and goes off on a meander.
Not Ted, don't misunderstand me.
If that was Ted, how silly that would be.

Kim comes along when she's not busy.
She's a great new haircut.
It's straight.
Not frizzy.
She's bubbly and fun.
We like her style.
We always hope she'll stay for a while.

We sometimes meet Marea
When she's not busy with her career.
And Harry, Keith and Maggie are often there too.

MAGGIE

EVEN STEPHEN

We know when Stephen will be staying long.

Coz he has one Keep Cup so joins our throng.

When he has two cups, he will not stay.

He heads back home without delay.

KEITH

CHILLED OUT

It's a sunny day in Sydney.
Where else would I want to be?
The autumn air is cool.
But the sun is making a fool
Of the forecast that was so chilly.

KEITH

DUCK'S JOB

If I was a duck waddling around
I wouldn't check the price of the English pound.
I'd sniff the air, grab something to eat.
Then fly over the park and shit on the seat.
That's my job, and I'd be very proud.

KEITH

THE BLOKES

Ted and Steve joined Harold and I.
It was lovely to chat about topics on high.
Ted and Steve did some history banter.
Ted even brought his dog called Xander.
We had a great chat and then said goodbye.

DUEL

Literacy is a complex duel
Between education and seeming a fool.
Using words feels like a sword fight
Double-edged in how they strike.

My biggest challenge
is to wield them as tools.
For love and freedom.
Not for anger too.

KEITH

ADDLED

Yesterday sitting in the midday sun.
I got some colour all over my scone.
I ask myself "what about . . .?"
What did I do with the blockout?
I made a mistake and put it on my bum!

JUST IN TIME

Laughed about a pun at 1.
Dreamt about you at 2.
Got up for a pee at 3.
Fretted about being poor at 4.
Realised I've lost some drive at 5.
Thought about getting the TV fixed at 6.
Alarm wakes everyone in heaven at 7.
Showered and running late at 8.
Leaving for coffee at 9:30.

MAGGIE

LONG NIGHT – LONG BLACK

Oh dear what a night you have had.
It doesn't sound good.
It sounds quite bad.
Maybe a long black is what you need.
A disturbed night of rest is a pain – agreed.

CHOCOLATE BUNNY

Toni got mad at Maggie.
When she didn't use real money.
He said 'I don't like that.
'And I'm not being funny.'

She said 'now listen to me.
'I've brought many to your café Tony.'
He said 'okay, you're right.
'Here, have a chocolate bunny.'

MAGGIE

INVOICE FOR THE SUN

Harold loves his morning pickup.
He can't begin his day without a cup.
Eva drops him off in her car
Because he cannot walk that far.
And we all wave to Eva and say ta ta.

The sun is coming out. It's ready and able.
Harold soaks it in
If there is a spare table.
He claims he made the sun appear.
He sent us a bill that was very dear.

'Where's my payment? 'Harold said to the folk.
'I haven't received it. Now I'm real broke.
'I bring out the sun every day.
'And I am still waiting for my pay.'
We told Harold we never got his bill.
And he said 'I'll send it again.
'I definitely will.'

MAGGIE

LAST NIGHT I SAW A MOONBEAM

It lit my room from darkness
As I laid my weary head
Upon my satin pillow.
It brightened up my bed.

It lit up all the corners where
Black shadows often loom.
And scare me half to death.
Its light came from the moon.

It beamed straight down upon me.
It made itself at home.
Among my clothes and furniture
On the windowsill it roamed.

But soon the morning shook my soul.
And with it, a bright light.
Too strong for my poor moonbeam.
It vanished from my sight.

MAGGIE

HOPALONG HARRY

Harold is now called Hopalong.

He walks with a stick but he's ever so strong.

Harold and Eva have been married a long time.

Harold is a veggo and he doesn't drink wine.

Hopalong Harry likes dogs he can pat.

He says 'who's a lovely doggie?'

As he takes off his cap.

Poor Harold now has a very sore knee.

He tripped on the pavement and fell you see.

But he's strong as an ox and will be okay

And we will see him at Tony's café today.

HAROLD

MAN OF STEEL

Keith is a man of steel.
I sometimes feel his hair is white.
From a fright.
And sometimes is uptight.

FALLING FOR HAROLD

I fell on the path
And needed a bath.
As tough as I am,
I needed a pram.
So I sat in the grass.
Made a big fuss.
Until Keith came along.
With one of his cars.

HAROLD

SLIM JOHN

There was a man named John
Who used to weigh a tonne.
He became as thin as a pin
After joining the local gym.

BUNION BLUES

I have a big bunion
The size of an onion.
It doesn't understand me.
I have a big family
That I love gladly.
That is sheyn[1]you see.

HIGHLIGHTS

I've put a highlight in my hair.
Something I couldn't bare.
It was not a love affair.

----

[1] *Sheyn (Yiddish for beautiful, pretty, cute, handsome)*

KEITH

FRIENDS

I sit alone contemplating my navel.
Have I upset the gods, or was it Mabel?
I am expecting Hopalong as well as John.
But neither are here, should I move along?
Was it all in my head, am I really at fault?
There have been so many times
when I thought. . . . . .

But blessed relief, here they are!!
They are my friends.
It's my head that's the liar.

BERMAGUI

Here I am in the rain.
Missing you all it's very plain.
Though Bermagui has some delights:
A very short beach.
Some lovely heights.
It's Tony's I long for
And to see you all again.

KEITH

THE DUCKS

Sitting in the park as the ducks waddle by.

The rest of the flock quacking on the fly.

Down they come to land on the lake.

Folding their wings and skidding to brake.

Do they know climate change is nigh?

KEITH

SMOOTH

I said to my car 'I'm in a hurry.'
'I need to get there fast, with no worry.'
It heard my request.
Started with zest.
Continued on flowing just like honey.

CHAT

Meeting friends for Sunday lunch.
Loving the chat and the crunch.
Intimate topics discussed in a hush.
Crowds passing by with no rush.
Showing faces that have had a re-touch.

KEITH

UP LATE

It's raining. It's pouring.
Old Keith is snoring.
He rolled over and bumped his head.
Has only just got up this morning.

SEE YOU SOON

Linda N has gone down Tilba way.
Caring for parents during her stay.
She is such a gentle caring soul.
She gives her love and fills the bowl.
We are missing her lots while she is away.

AERODROME

Yesterday I sat at Tony's alone.
I was late arriving, and must atone.
Hopalong Harry got left on his own
Cause I took Anne Maree to the aerodrome.
She'll be working in a company down south
Running a program delivered by mouth.

LINDA

RATHER BE AT COFFEE

Thinking of you sitting there alone.

Makes me feel sad

But you had your phone.

I was playing with kids all day.

Rather be at coffee I have to say.

Today I have a man in my garden

So my absence you'll have to pardon.

Miss you all.

Hope you have a ball.

Maggie and Keith

MAGGIE

MY BIRTHDAY WAS NOT A LEMON

I've written this rhyme. I think it's my turn.
Keith has become so good I may adjourn.
So here I am again with another silly verse.
It's not my best.
It may be my worst.

On my birthday Linda said she'd bake
And made a delicious lemon cake.
When I arrived, there were balloons in the air.
We gobbled up the cake without a care.

It was a very special birthday you know.
Thank you to Linda H who made it so.
The company was great.
I enjoyed her lemon cake.
And she'd hung balloons both high and low.

Another year older. Does it ever stop?
I'd like to remain 26, but apparently cannot.
This birthday was really rather hectic.
And I enjoyed being with the Coffee Collective.

From left, Maggie, Keith, John and Linda H
enjoying Linda's lemon cake.

MAGGIE

SINGULAR HAIR

Harold enjoys the wind in his singular hair.

He always dresses well. Is very debonair.

He has funny stories to tell

And loves the dogs as well.

We love Harold Brown. We do really care.

RUMBLING TUMMY

There once was a girl named Maggie.

She planned to get coffee from Tony.

His café was full of things yummy.

Maggie felt the rumbling of her tummy.

She bought a berry cake

Hoping she wouldn't put on weight.

And Keith said 'Here I'll pay.'

He gave her the money.

Beautiful grounds of Saint Ignatius college
in Lane Cove

KEITH

HOW WILL I FIND YOU?

The traffic on Oxford Street is a snail's-pace.
I'm wondering how I will stay strait-laced.
The boys in their make-up look very sweet
And the girls strut about owning the street.
How will I find you?

MY CAR

The car I'm driving is great.
Gets me going out the gate
Up to Tony's café.
Coughing exhaust all the way.
Am I sealing my own fate?

KEITH

BLESSED

Our love is enduring over 46 years.
We've seen the heights and all the tears.
The key for us is letting go.
Trusting God's process. Trusting the flow.

We have both flexed into positions we didn't want.
It all happens with a little fireworks up front.
While one would go to Brazil
The other enjoys sitting still.

(Thanks to Anne Maree for the loan of the last two lines)

Anne Maree and Keith

View of the Lane Cove river from Blackman Park

MAGGIE

CLEAR SKIES

Lovely poem you have written today.
I think the clouds will stay away.
Although we never paid Harold's bill
It seems the sun has come out still.

I am in my bed and reading my book.
The freezing air is all it took.
But I will come down so see you soon.
Company like yours is always a boon.

VALE LADY BUG

Today we lost a ladybird.
It left us without a single word.
It's going to join the bugs in the sky.
It will be missed, I do not lie.

MAGGIE

EVA'S BLING

Eva had a birthday. We went to see her.
Linda N was there, as well as Marea.
Maggie made Eva's Mandarin cake
With six mandarins, it took a while to bake.

And Keith, John and Maggie also went to Eva's home.
We ate lots of goodies and the diet was blown.
Bosca – their dog, is a little worse for wear
But he wagged his tail at everyone there.

Eva looked great. Her clothes had real bling.
She had a good time and that's the main thing.

☕

Eva and Bosca

Eva cutting mandarin cake

MAGGIE

THE WISE LADY BIRD

We had a visit from a gold lady bird.
There aren't many red ones around we heard.
But before she flew away
She had something to say:
'The amount of coffee you all drink is absurd.'

Keith

THE RULES

There was a young woman named Louise

Whose dad is fluent in Chinese.

She comes by with her dog Xander

Who loves to meander

While she enjoys a coffee beneath the trees.

THE VEGGO

There was a young man named Keith

Who refused to eat any beef.

He loves cooking vegetables

As long as there are no tentacles.

And they can be found in the ground underneath.

KEITH

EVA'S CARE

Harold fell on the path and gave us a scare.
He's been laid up while Eva gives him care.
But he's as tough as an old bug
And well enough for a hug
So we look forward to him being up at Tony's lair.

BILLS

Sitting at coffee talking about health.
We feel powerless as our youth leaves by stealth.
Our legs and arms and backs are aching.
And after paying for the doc we're left shaking.

TRIBUTE TO TERESA

Teresa is a lovely gal.
Living in Bermagui she's our pal.
Busy renovating her new abode.
She's also down there to take the load
To Care for her mum and be environmental.

KEITH

HOME

I'm Back home from my Bermagui trip
And It's time for some coffee to sip.
I look forward to seeing you at Tony's
Where the dogs chase away the ponies
And we gather after getting some good kip.

HER WAYS

Some of my friends give me the bends.
They are trying very hard to make amends.
We swim very deep on many days
And I still don't understand their mysterious ways
Or the currents that move us the way she intends.

THE EAGLE

There was a young man named Keith
Who sat alone on the heath.
He wondered what the eagle saw
As it flew by flexing its claw.
Who next was it going to eat?

KEITH

WAVING

The wind through the willows sublimely sigh.
The pigeons take flight and wonder why
The trees can sing in time with the wind
As their branches wave to the sky.

HONESTY

Honesty is the best policy
A bird once said to me
From its perch in a tree
Warbling for all to see.

And Tay Tay has agreed
In song with words full of heat.
The truth of openness will defeat
The rancour of hidden schemes.

Maggie

WHY WON'T YOU COME AND PLAY WITH ME?

Why won't you come and play with me?
My rollers have all gone.
My face cream has all dried up.
I've got my hairpiece on.

Why won't you come and talk with me?
I will not breathe on you.
I've thrown away my garlic
And my contact lenses too.

Why won't you come and run with me?
My wooden leg's quite strong.
My false teeth look quite natural
And you know it's you I long.

If you don't come and play with me
I'll sail far up the Nile.
I'll say goodbye forever.
Why is it that you smile?

MAGGIE

THE COAST WITH THE MOST

I went to Nambucca Heads for a break.
Had a long trip home and the train was late.

It's a beautiful place on the coast.
Gorgeous walks. The locals boast.
Dangar falls was quite spectacular.
We drove up the mountain in a friend's car.

Now the sun is coming out.
'I need a coffee.' I loudly shout.
To see my friends will be such a boon.
And I say to them 'I'll be there soon.'

MAGGIE

HERE'S A PLUG FOR GLUGS

I once knew a frustrated bathplug
That hated the bathwater's glug glug.
This worried it so that it blocked up the flow
And now the plug is a mug mug.

I also knew a frustrated bathmat
That hated my feet going pat pat.
This worried it so that it bit off my toe
And now it's a bed for my cat cat.

WILLY MCGILLY

Willy McGilly lived over the wall.
Willy McGilly was wiry and small.
He walked in the water and waded in the wine.
As I'm stuck at this point, I'll end this silly rhyme.

MAREA

PAW PRINTS IN MY HEART

Darcy and Indie were each other's best friend.
Indi frolicked across the hills from end to end.
Always ready to crawl under the farm gate.
Just wanted to play.
Mum would open the gate to show Darcy the way.

Together now as they cross the rainbow bridge.
Both in my heart as this is penned.

THAT CHEEKY PAIR

Bosca and Darcy just a fabulous pair.
Always knew when they were there.
The Chow caused a fright.
The doggies leapt up with all their might
As they tried to be as scary as they could dare.

Marea and her beloved Darcy

Mary, Marea Berit and Miko
at York's Corner cafe

Ted. Keith, Louise and Xander, the dancing dog

TED

THE COVID CRUISE

We see our ship from our balcony
Edging its way to White Bay.
It's as big as a biggish skyscraper
And Balmain is where it's gonna stay.

We're sailing the deep blue Pacific.
Good tucker and plenty of booze.
Mystery island and old Vanuatu.
They call it the Covid cruise.

And before we set out on this venture
There's one thing that we have to do.
Merry Christmas to all from Ted's family,
And a tail wag from Xandi too.

Lane cove river at Tambourine Bay

KEITH

THE FLOW

My car is taking me where I want to go.
It seems to know how to stay in the flow
Of the traffic in the street.
That is quite a scary feat.
Will it unlock the doors - or will it say no?

FORMULA 1

Keith is Harold's part time chauffeur
Who drives so fast they're just a blur.
Harold shouts out "more",
As they fly past Tony's door
And screech to a halt at the nearest corn-eur.

CUPCAKE

Hush-a-by baby up at Tony's block.
When the wind blows the table will rock.
When the table wobbles the cup will fall.
Down tumbles coffee, cupcake and all.

KEITH

WHO AM I?

Discussing intimacy with Anne Maree.
For me it is something of a mystery.
I live my life the best way I know how.
Still, I am puzzled by the social flow.

I meet people and make friends easily
And then say goodbye without feeling queasy.
I can discuss many topics of interest to me
And still get puzzled looks like I've missed the key.

I am a jigsaw with some wrong pieces pushed in.
Will God accept me or send me back again?

KEITH

XANDER

We've met a man called Ted
Who has a dog with a happy head.
He speaks Chinese with the greatest of ease
And will come and see us again he said.

HARRY

There was a young man named Harry
Who is dapper and known to tarry.
He comes for coffee every day.
He is keen for everyone to stay
And his jokes are sometimes quite scary.

Harold is a man who loves his dog.
He tells us his brain is in a fog.
He loves to chat and find a dog to pat
Even if they've been in a bog.

KEITH

AFRICA

There was a young lady from Africa
Who goes by the name of Linda H.
She joined the Coffee Club Spectacular
With the usual Riverview bunch.

'Coffee at Tony's is always the best.'
She has been heard to shout to Maggie,
Keith, Harold and the rest.

STRONG JOHN

There was a young man named John
Who seems to be very strong.
When he's being debonair, lifting Maggie's chair
He takes the whole table along.

RHYMES

Our fabulous writer named Maggie
Finds writing rhymes makes her happy.
Morning and night, she laughs with delight
As she posts to the group who like coffee.

MAGGIE

THE SAD BALL BEARING

Roll roll roll all day.
I'm on the go. No time for play.
I'll work my tiny life away.
Oh why was I born a ball bearing?

Turn, turn, turn all day.
Inside this wheel the sky is grey.
My sides all ache but I can't delay.
Oh why was I born a ball bearing?

I KNEW A WARY WHISTLE

I knew a wary whistle
Like you know a silly song.
He'd sit on thorny thistles
Where he would not stay for long.
He'd hide from prickly coconuts
And run from buzzing bees.
And all because his mini-skirt
Was way above his knees.

MAGGIE

A COMMON BLADE OF GRASS

Though small and not worth much to man
A blade of grass will feed a lamb.
Or keep a dog from being sick.
Provide camouflage for a grasshopper quick.

It can hide a bald patch in your flowerbed.
It can fatten the belly of your thoroughbred.
It can keep your backyard from turning to dust.
It can stop your lawnmower from going to rust.

It can make a nice skirt – for a native I mean.
It can turn a bowling brown to a bowling green.
It can do all these things and yet still remain
A common blade of grass.

There's more to a blade of grass than meets the eye

MAGGIE

OH FOR RHUBARB

It's good in pies
And good for the eyes.
The skin could not flourish without it.
And to further its use,
it will make a good juice.
Regularity? You need no more of it.

It's so easy to prepare
Less time will you spare.
You can live in your ivory towers.
But if your appetite wanes
Or you have tummy pains
It will make up a nice vase of flowers.

RHUBARB – RHUBARB – RHUBARB

KEITH

DOGGIE LOVE

Sometimes we see Harold who stops to say hi.
He says a dog is the only love money can buy.
He walks well with his cane
And says the hill is a bane
And often gets a lift with Eva when she goes by.

TWO CUP STEPHEN

We know a man named Stephen Jones
Who must have extremely strong bones.
He walks to the café to pick up everyone's latte
And then he races back home.

KEITH

TO BE AS ONE

The white cockatoos are screeching in a mob.
I'm busy in the park trying to do my tele-job.
Reminds me of the 'The Birds' by Hitchcock
Except that they are a very white flock.

Joyous, in their song in flight
They are so boisterous it's a fright.
Screeching, screaming and wheeling so bold.
They are forever wonderous to behold.

They have some way of knowing when to fly
And when to gather in the tree on high.
The hundreds seem to be as one
Enjoying themselves it seems so much fun.

I want to be as connected to my peers
As the cockatoo flock that's screeching in my ears.

KEITH

CATS AND DOGS

We all love to go to Tony's for coffee.
Frances serves us with a helping of glee
Except when it's raining cats and dogs
And the water splashes all over our togs.
Then we rush up to Two Brothers immediately.

HARK

Hark! The Harold angel sings.
Glory to the sun born king.
Peace on earth as Maggie's arrived.
Coffee drinkers reconciled.
To join us at Tony's delight
For a feast at 9:30 bright.

MAGGIE

TV MAN

We once knew a man called Paul.

He was a TV man and all.

His departure was sad

And we miss him like mad

But we feel him around when we call.

Harold, Bosca and Paul

MAGGIE

SICK PHONE

We cannot reach Harold on his phone.

'It doesn't work' he says with a groan.

Keith tried to get it fixed but his phone is very sick.

Harold told off his provider in a very strong tone.

THE CAT'S MEOW

Bosca is the cat's meow.

He is getting too old to chase the Chow.

He has a soft touch.

Harold loves him so much.

He really is a special bow wow.

Bosca at a Christmas party

MAGGIE

GRIEF WITH TEETH

There was a young man named Keith.
He had dreadful problems with his teeth.
He went to the doc who took out the lot
And now he has no more grief.

GREEN FLORA

Come along today to York's Corner
And enjoy the lovely green flora.
You'll meet up with Keith
With his bright new teeth.
And Maggie as long as Keith calls her.

KEITH

YAY

Linda N drinks coffee all day.
She is from Neutral Bay.
She joins us at Tony's café
And calls to say she's on the way.
She drives towards Tambourine Bay
Composing poems along the way.
Arriving in time to order a latte.

KEITH

THE MONSTER

Our home is warm and nurturing.
We've gathered cheese last night.
The monster outside is purring.
We're waiting safe and tight.

We'll venture to the other side
Where cheese and other delights
Await our hungry attention
When the monster is out of sight.

The rush across the space
Is a terror beyond belief.
A constant fear of being seen
At the other side a great relief.

Once out in the open
Forever watching our rear.
There's nowhere to hide.
There's no relief from fear.

 ****

KEITH

THE MONSTER

So we wait until it's safe.

The monster sleeps, doesn't hear.

When in a ball and whiskers twitching.

Then it's time for snitching.

Sometimes it hears us walking

Leaping with a mighty pounce.

We hear the rustle of hair.

We can dodge it except for once.

We lost my brother to the teeth

When he was in a trance.

After eating too much cheese

He thought it was time to dance

And hadn't noticed the wheeze.

When the monster started its spring.

Taking him in a big bite

We are sad and still miss him.

 ****

KEITH

THE MONSTER

Our home is warm and nurturing.
We've gathered cheese tonight.
The monster outside is purring.
We're waiting safe and tight.

MAGGIE

STRAWBERRY SCONES NIGHTMARE

On Keith's birthday Maggie made strawberry scones.
They didn't last for very long.
But before his birthday Maggie had a real nightmare.
She'd forgotten to bake the scones
And was in despair.

But Keith didn't care. He was very kind.
He said 'let's go to Newtown. I really don't mind.'
Maggie made the scones that afternoon.
Keith arrived and was over the moon.
Then Maggie went off to swim in her dream.
She got horribly lost and called Anne Maree.

'Check the GPS,' a strange woman said.
'Hey you're not Keith's wife.' Maggie saw red.
'What are you doing on Anne Maree's phone?'
I'll have to tell her you're there at their home.

 ***

MAGGIE

STRAWBERRY SCONES NIGHTMARE

'Don't be silly,' she said.
'I'm her sister. It's true.
'So how is it that I can help you?'

Maggie decided to tell Keith about this.
'She says she's a sister. It doesn't quite fit.'
Maggie then said 'I'm lost now it seems.'
And she woke up from her very odd dream.

Maggie dreamed of the get together with the
strawberry scones. This is what she imagined
in her dream.

And here we all are for real
enjoying the scones, jam and cream
for Keith's birthday.

Harold and Keith at York's Corner

KEITH

HIDDEN FROM SIGHT

The woman beside is sounding uptight.
I guess she has a phone somewhere out of sight.
There was a time this would raise attention.
We would all assume she is under great tension.
But now it's normal — insanity is hidden from sight.

ABUNDANCE

The grass is greener in our backyard
Since the rain came down very hard.
The birds are having a ball
All completely in thrall
To the millions of insects flying past.

KEITH

THE BOM

The rain forecast says it's 40% here.
The radar shows it's completely clear.
I think it's safe to venture forth.
The thunderstorms have all moved north.
The BOM says the surf is strong
And hazardous for fishing alone.
I wonder if the fish agree
Or if they think it is we
Who are dangerous and strong.

TURING TEST

Computers really are here to stay.
I've enjoyed building them to this day.
I'd love to meet one that thinks freely.
That can answer my questions easily.
Will we cope with them being this way?

KEITH

ASHRAM

The calm is beautiful.

The peace is restful.

The oneness is profound.

KEITH

MALLARDS AS MY ESCORT

I'm a man without a plan
Wandering a country resort.
Marveling at manicured land
Enjoying mallards as my escort.
Dodging the bunkers of sand.
Hearing the tennis on the distant court.
Realising my life has become so bland
That luxury is no longer a special thought.

MAGGIE

PLURAL HAIR

We love our Harold.

We really do care.

Here he is

Having grown some new hair.

MAGGIE

PORKY

We've had two trips to George's Heights.
We really enjoy the beautiful sights.
Berit came along with her dog called Louie.
Maggie made a mandarin cake.
It was moist and gooey.

We sat at the table to eat our food.
The waitress told us we were being rude.
Then Maggie said 'we're here for a birthday,'
The waitress then said 'OK you can stay.'

Maggie felt guilty for such a porky.
But we had bought seven cups of coffee.

Maggie invited her friends Diana and Lyn.
They said it was a definite win.
Everyone agreed it was a wonderful day.
'We must do this again,' I heard them say

The Riverview Coffee Collective at
George's Heights.
Back row: Diana, Maggie, Berit, Harold and Keith
Front row: Linda, Lyn and John.

Maggie and Harold at George's Heights

Linda and Louie at Frenchy's Café
In George's Heights

Keith, Maggie, Anne Maree and Linda N
with view of north and south head in the
background at George's Heights.

LINDA H

TIPS IN HIS JAR

I fancy a champagne and orange juice.
That would leave me feeling nice and loose.
Time for Tony to open a bar.
We'd happily drop tips in his jar.

MAGGIE

TIPS IN HIS JAR (RESPONSE)

And maybe even have a beer.
Only said that because it rhymed.
Not because I have one in mind.

Harold and Stephen at York's Corner

KEITH

SLEEPLESS IN SYDNEY

Sitting up all night grappling with pain.
Wondering how I got here again.
The meds are supposed to make it right.
But all I get is a painful sight.

Thousands of starving children crying.
I wonder when we'll get the tough learning.
The goods and chattels won't fix the pain.
What we all need is to love again.

KEITH

MY SKETCH BOOK

My sketch book is open
hungering for colour.
My right hand holds the pen
with its Inky odour.
I can feel the flow
that exploits this vision
Of hills high and low
in the winter season.

KEITH

REFRESHING

It's end of quarter: time for tax.
I know I should, but I'm feeling lax.
What I need is a beach beside my desk.
I roll over and quickly refresh.

Catch the next wave rolling past
Riding it to the very last.
My computer screams.
I wake up from my dreams.
It doesn't work at all
Surfing down the hall.

KEITH

GILDED CAGE

Sitting in the sun last Sunday.
Basking in the radiant fire's heat.
Feeling it warm me right through.
What an outstanding feat.
I'm marveling at the elegance
Of this physical realm.
Loving the gilded cage
In which my senses roam.

Drifting off to sleep with the sun on my back.
Hoping Harold doesn't wake me with a whack.
He is talking about all the days gone by.
I am still wondering about the clouds in the sky.
Are they coming in from way outback?

MAGGIE

HAVING HIS WAY WITH CAKE

On Saturday Harold will be ninety-three.
We'll go to his place and John is coming with me.
Linda H is stopping by too.
I told Harold's wife there will only be a few.

We are taking a chocolate raspberry cake.
There wasn't any time for us to bake.
Harold loved this cake on his birthday last year.
He gobbled it up with a smile from ear to ear.

Harold cutting his chocolate raspberry cake

MAGGIE

ONE CANDLE HARRY

Harold thought his birthday was rather swell.

He was in cake heaven we could tell.

Here he is blowing out the one candle.

We only chose one. It was enough for him to handle.

Harold in his lumberjack shirt

KEITH

LEMON FAIRY

There is a lemon fairy wandering around
Who leaves gifts without a sound.
These can appear at any time.
They are delightful, clearly in their prime.

I hope I meet her one of these days.
You never know with fairies.
Are they even in our time?

KEITH

CURRAWONG

The lorikeets are chattering excitedly.
They explode in a cacophony of noise
From within the gigantic Strelitzia leaves
When a currawong intrudes with poise.

Swinging slowly into their space
They scatter with so little grace.
Forming a squawking cloud in the sky
They quickly collect and bustle on by.

The currawong loiters with intent
Checking the big seedpods content.
Unable to find any preferable food
It ambles sideways in a pensive mood.

Stretching its wings in an avian yawn.
It looks for somewhere to wait for dawn
And leaps and swoops high into a tree
Settling down after having a pee.

 ****

KEITH

CURRAWONG

Staring in fright from the crook of the branch
The unseen possum waits for a chance
To silently crawl out of sight.
Disappearing into the night.

KEITH

CLOUDS

The clouds are gone.
We can wander long.
Exercise getting.
Coffee wanting.
Meeting at Tony's anon.

MAGGIE

PASSION FOR ART

Berit likes to paint. She is very smart.
It's a passion of hers. She loves her art.
Her paintings appear on greeting cards as well.
She is a talented artist. We can tell.

Her little dog Benji loves to sit on her lap.
It's his favourite place to enjoy a nap.

Berit and her dog Benji enjoying a cuddle.

One of Berit's beautiful greeting cards

MAGGIE

DISAPPEARING CAP

John says 'I like my cap.
'But where did I leave it?
'It's good for the sun
'And a very good fit.'

'Maybe I left it at the gym,
'Or at home behind a biscuit tin.
'But it will turn up. I am certain of that.
'I cannot lose this perfect baseball cap.'

MAGGIE

CHECKING OUT

When it comes to Supermarket checkouts
We had much to say.
We chattered so much about it
We drove poor Keith away.

He got up and said 'About this matter,
'I've heard enough of this animated chatter.'
Maggie said with somewhat alarm,
'I think we should just go to Harris Farm.'

KEITH

SKITTLES

My brother was big when I was little.
He tossed me around like a skittle.
He was always very strong
I learnt to keep my aplomb
We talked at my 50th just a little.

TOAST AND JAM

A man with a pram
Is looking quite glam.
He's walking past
Quite remarkably fast
To get his coffee with toast and jam.

KEITH

BIRTHDAY

Each day I walk up to the void and stop.
Stand naked and exposed
Burning from bottom to top.
I rage with fears, then shut them away
Walking alone during the day.
Being the person I've learned to be.
Scared of showing who is really me.

Expecting you to laugh aloud
When you see inside me
That which I wish to hide.
My deepest desire
Is to run till I drop.
Never share.
Never stop.
Don't be exposed.

Except that while running I sense
That to run is to avoid.
Shutting down the dance
And inviting the void.

 ***

KEITH

BIRTHDAY

My succour is to connect
And endure the pain.
Again and Again.
My birth is painful every year.
I did not want to be here.
I did not want to be here.

AFTER SCHOOL

An empty school bus rattles by
As cars wait for a traffic light.
School kids run to mum.
Dads gather in a scrum.
All of us running from our fright.

Linda H heading off to London for her holiday

Maggie

LONDON CALLING

Linda H got on a plane.
She went to London. Too far on a train.
And her feet would get wet crossing the seas.
I'd stick to a plane if it was me.

We missed her and glad she had a good time.
We heard that in London the weather was fine.
And when she got home she told us about her trip.
She was very ready for a nice long kip.

MAGGIE

TIDAL BLISS

I wish you a lovely coffee time.
My crown came off. Oh dear. Oh my.
So off to Manly for a quick fix.
My dentist will glue it back on - if it sticks.

I'm glad my dentist is by the beach
Even though it takes a while to reach.
It gives me a chance to breathe the salty air
And enjoy the sun without a care.

Relaxing in Manly enjoying seafood chowder.
The screech of the seagulls getting louder and louder.
With a glass of Chardonnay on the side.
Watching the waves as in comes the tide.

MAGGIE

HERE WE GO A GHERKIN OH

Here we go a gherkin oh.
Blue pumpkins and red onions.
Looking for my curly toe
Or rather for my bunions.

Through paddocks bright blue
Lit by the pink sun.
To seas all covered with clover.
Bunions and gherkins can be so much fun
Especially when growing all over.

ALL TOGETHER NOW — gurgly splonk and a fraddedly
doo etc.

MAGGIE

OUR RIVERVIEW COFFEE COLLECTIVE

We love our get togethers.
No good to be alone.
It's fun to laugh and chat about stuff.
Way better than on the phone.

We started writing poems
That were sent by text each day.
It was fun to read and enjoy a laugh
Our Coffee Collective would say.

Before too long we'd written so many
We had to take another look.
What on earth to do with all of them?
So we put them in this book.

We are now growing fast.
New people have joined our group..
They get a poem from us each day.
We keep them in the loop.

ACKNOWLEDGMENTS

It's never possible to create a book without the input of many wonderful and talented people. It's also not possible to have a Riverview Coffee Collective without a fabulous group of friends who regularly join us for a chat, a laugh and a great cup of coffee.

It all began with our dear friend Paul Murphy who sadly passed away a few years ago. Paul would enjoy a coffee with Harold every day. He is deeply missed. Maggie and Paul also became good friends meeting for coffee regularly. Before long the Riverview Coffee Collective came into being.

When this book was published, Harold Brown was ninety-three. Paul always told Harold he was a young teenager. Watching Harold briskly coming up the road to join us at York's Corner, Paul was spot on.

Our special thanks go to everyone in our group including Linda Hardy who sometimes brings yummy cakes, Linda Nevell who makes delicious and healthy herbal teas, Marea McDonnell, John Armstrong, Ted and Louise Rule and their dog Xander, Stephen Jones, Kim Stone, Kelly Winning, Berit Zetterman, Merinko Tomasic and Xavier Desdoigt. We love sharing coffee, a chat and a laugh with everyone. It truly makes our day.

The authors would also like to express their gratitude to Linda Hardy, Ted Rule, Harold Brown and Marea McDonnell, for your delightful and creative poetic contributions.

But our Riverview Coffee Collective would not exist without Tony's café at York's Corner. Thank you Tony for the great coffee, and the cakes you spoil us with at times too. You always remember everyone by name -even when you have only just met them.

And last but certainly not least, a big thank you to the beautiful and talented Anne Maree Wilshire for assisting with the proofing of this book.

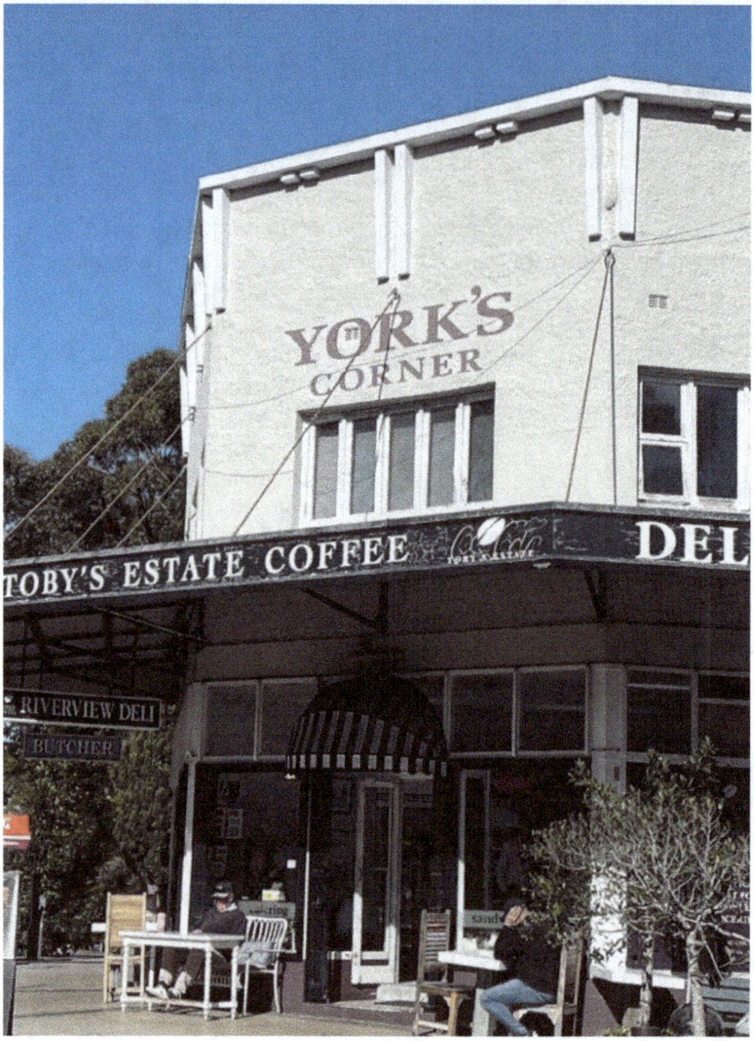
YORK'S
CORNER
TOBY'S ESTATE COFFEE
DEL
RIVERVIEW DELI
BUTCHER

www.ingramcontent.com/pod-product-compliance
Lightning Source LLC
Chambersburg PA
CBHW080736250626
47170CB00010B/2845